#Expert

The Business Owner's Guide To Building Authority On Social Media

Meliss Jakubovic

Download all resources at
www.HashtagExpertBook.com/resources

ISBN: 9781790658336

Cover Design and Artwork: Jade Smith
Interior Design: Meliss Jakubovic
Cover and Author Photography: Alicia A. Kozak

Edited by: Roberta Markevitch, Shayla Penman

Kindle Direct Publishing- KDP

Kindle Direct Publishing
410 Terry Avenue North
Seattle, WA 98109

DEDICATION

For the hustlers, entrepreneurs, believers, dreamers, doers, implementors, and game-changers, this is for you. You have what it takes to be crazy enough to make changes in this world. Somebody's gotta do it and way to go you, for taking the first steps. You've got this.

Contents

ACKNOWLEDGMENTS

Thank you to Roberta Markevitch for always believing in me and for the endless support. You mean the world to me. I'd like to thank my two boys, Shai and Ilan for choosing me as their Ima and always getting excited with me when big things happen in my business. You watch my growth with big eyes and encouragement and you give my life purpose. I also enjoy encouraging you through your entrepreneurial endeavors and I always will. Thank you to my dad, George Jay for always believing in my abilities and standing by my decisions. I appreciate you. And a huge thank you goes to my team. I am only able to do what I do because of how hard you all work to help make it happen. Much love and admiration for all of you. I also want to thank everyone who has supported me online: my followers, fans, and subscribers. This whole operation wouldn't be possible or purposeful without all of you.

CHAPTER ONE
MY STORY

I'm sitting in the LAX airport writing this after traveling here last minute for a 1-day conference to accelerate my business. You see, I'm an implementer. When I feel that it's time to grow, I find the perfect person to take me there, I do what they tell me to do, and I implement it faster than Superman can fly across the world. Well, maybe not that fast but I couldn't resist the opportunity to use Superman in my book 'cause I was obsessed with Superman as a child.

Superman... It's amazing how many times the idea of a superhero has continuously come up in my life. My dad has overcome 11 surgeries; from heart surgery to stomach surgery, several cancers, and everything in between. I'm a holocaust survivor grandchild and I have had my share of tough situations so #hero and #survivor have come up a lot in my life.

After my divorce, I became a single mom on Welfare, barely scraping by knowing that I was meant for greatness. My two boys deserved everything in this world and I wanted to be the one to provide it for them. To me, a SuperPERSON is someone who can keep going when times are tough, someone who can see the big picture and work their ass off to get there. A person who doesn't allow anyone or any situation to stand in their way. They cut through the noise, negativity, and doubt from everyone around them and even from themselves. A Superperson is a person that is meant for greatness and implements whatever strategies or solutions it takes to make it to that goal. They are someone who doesn't stop, no matter what because they can see that it's all about the end-game. The long-haul. It's all about moving the needle day-in and day-out and that is exactly what I did.

This book isn't about how I became a Facebook Ad Expert and Online Marketing Strategist. It's not about how I run a leading marketing agency from my bedroom in my PJ's. It's not about how I manage multi-million-dollar brands and was featured in Forbes twice for my social media expertise, or how I founded the Social Marketing Academy to teach business owners how to market their products and services effectively online.

This book is about you! It's about how you can position yourself as an authority on social media, so you too can impact the world and make your dreams come true.

If you picked up this book you probably own a business and want to understand how to make it successful using proven social marketing tactics. You have probably tried before and failed, or you are just starting out and want to do it right from the get-go (Way to go you, Rockstar!). But whatever it is that got you here, I want to congratulate you for taking this step towards becoming the Superperson that you are, an implementer, a dreamer, a creator, a go-getter. You can build the authority you need to skyrocket your business and I'm gonna show you how.

I've been featured on countless stages, radio programs, podcasts, TV segments, and guest blogs. I've learned through trial, error, and some amazing top coaches and influencers just how to get what I want and that's what I want to share with you.

Times have been challenging. There have been plenty of times where I felt like I was about to break. I wasn't even sure if it made sense to carry on with my business because the effort and the countless hours I put in never seemed to equal the pay at the end of the day. But it all comes down to this: If you know that what you have to offer is valuable and you know that you can help people and serve others in your industry, it's time to come to the realization (if you haven't already) that you have a purpose and what you have to offer is important and needs to be seen by the masses.

If you have gotten this far, you know it's time to build your authority and do what you are meant to do. So enough chit-chat. Let's build your authority and get you the visibility you deserve because the world can't wait any longer for what you provide!

CHAPTER TWO
AUTHORITY POSITIONING

Now it's time to position you as the authority in your industry. Does that excite you? Or does that scare you?

If you aren't used to being the center of attention or you have no preparation, that may sound a bit scary but don't worry, I'm gonna walk you through it. In order for you to be the go-to person, you have to set yourself up that way. It's an essential part of growing your business because without authority, there is no compelling reason to buy from you over someone else.

The first thing I tell all my clients is that they need professional pictures. If you are a coach or consultant, social media manager, VA, doctor, author, course creator, blogger, etc... basically, if you are a service-based business, you need to be the face of your business, so you will need professional pictures of yourself.

Imagine going to a website for a great service you are interested in only to find selfie pictures and some awkward, cropped photos. You know, the ones with 2 people in the photo with 1 cropped out, so you see the person's face at a weird angle, or maybe a hand on their shoulder coming out of nowhere

Now, imagine going to a website of another company that offers the same thing and you see high-quality, professional photos in great lighting.

Service-based business:

No cut-outs or selfies.

Yes to professional photos in good
lighting.

Product-based business:

No poorly lit iPhone photos.

Yes to professional photos in good lighting.

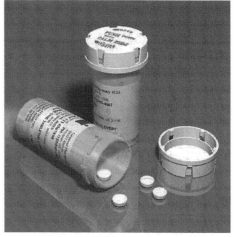

(Higher quality images can be found at HashtagExpertBook.com/resources)

Which company will you instantly feel that you can trust? The one with the professional photos, obviously!

If you have a product that you sell, like jewelry, makeup, supplements... you need to have professional photos of your products! Don't expect people to buy from you if all your pictures look like a Craigslist ad or a garage sale post. Take your business seriously and get professional photos!

To position yourself as the authority, you need to really show up that way and professional pictures are the first thing your audience will see, so make sure they are high-quality and in good lighting.

In order to create authority in your audience, you need to focus on a niche. What is your zone of genius? Some of the biggest business mistakes I see are people trying to be a jack-of-all-trades. The problem with this is that they end up having a watered-down brand and are masters of nothing.

I run a complete online marketing agency, but I specialize in Facebook ads and sales funnels. This means that since I've been in the community a while now; when people think of a FB ad expert, they think of Meliss Marketing... Me. I'm actually known in the industry as the "Lead Generation Genie". So, when you are thinking about your industry, think about how you want to be known and how you'd like to be referred by others.

Ask yourself these questions to help you niche down:

What gaps need to be filled in my industry?

What unique skill-set or value can I provide to my clients and customers?

What problems or needs do my existing customers share with me?

What is my dream client's biggest challenge?

A good way to get the answers to these questions is to research! I have a folder of questions on my computer that people have asked me; in emails, as comments on blogs, posts, live videos, and on phone conversations. I can always refer back to this folder when I'm thinking of content that I need to create for my market.

Ask your audience lots of questions. Be very specific and when they answer you, try to get even more specific. See what they need in their business and what their setbacks and obstacles are.

For example, one week I asked my audience, "What is your biggest struggle in your business?" A lot of people said, "confidence". Well, I wanted them to be extremely specific, so I asked, "Confidence in what?" Once they started answering me in detail, I gained incredible insight into their pain points: fearing rejection, not knowing how to represent themselves, doubting their business, lacking confidence in sales.

Once you have determined your niche, you'll want to provide lots of value. Share your knowledge in the places where your community is spending the most time. For example, if you help people write job resumes, you probably don't want to be spending a lot of time on Snapchat. Your ideal market will most likely be on LinkedIn. So, figure out where your market is hanging out and be there, consistently. You need to show up every day. I challenge you to do this 30 minutes a day for 30 days:

Sign on to the platform of your choice and set a timer for 30 minutes. Comment on posts and connect with as many people as possible until the timer goes off. Make sure you are offering valuable advice and information with each comment. This is how you start a snowball effect, just by adding value everywhere you can. This is only the beginning. There are many ways to pick up traffic, so be consistent. You will see by the end of the 30 days that you'll have lots of engagement and will have built many new relationships to get that snowball to start rolling!

When I say "provide value": I mean that you should not be selling anything. You want to give and give and give some more on the front-end because people are more likely to buy from those they know, like, and trust, and that doesn't happen overnight. To provide value, you need to understand what is meaningful to your ideal market. What you may find valuable may not be what your market needs, so be in tune-with their needs and ask a lot of questions.

I want you to think: "What's in it for them?" And also pay special attention to the type of content your market likes to consume. Do they like live video? Podcasts? Blogs? Articles? Images? A good rule of thumb is to mix it up but if you notice a type of content that gets better engagement than another, it's a good thing to note.

So, "What's in it for them?" Create content that will be the most helpful for them and provide the most value such as infographics, podcasts, video series', webinars, reports, checklists, etc. If you need content ideas, you can look at my course "How To Create A Killer Content Calendar" inside the academy. Download all resources at www.HashtagExpertBook.com/resources

The 30 minutes for 30 days challenge will help you be consistent. Consistency establishes your reputation as an authority and builds trust because it allows your audience to know that you are not just going to take their money and run. You are reliable and professional and an expert in your industry that they can trust to show up again and again with lots of value.

So, figure out what your niche is and what you are going to talk about. Then stick to your brand so you are easily identifiable. Use the same fonts and colors everywhere. Put your logo on everything you produce. When people are ready to come to you to solve their problems, they know exactly how to find you and can relate to your brand that they already know, like, and trust.

Before we head over to the next chapter, I just want to reiterate how important it is to build relationships everywhere you go. Engage with your community. Find out what's important to them. Celebrate their wins along the way. Connect with experts and influencers in your field to expand your reach and gain social proof of your work.

Positioning yourself as an authority isn't hard but it certainly is step 1 in having a booming business, so take it seriously. Be consistent, put on your big girl/boy pants because it can be a little bit scary, but continue to learn, continue to implement, and never stop providing value.

Provide Value: Are You Offering Help Everywhere You Go?
Give and give and give some more on the front end.

Be Consistent: Do The 30 Minutes For 30 Days Challenge

Set a timer for 30 minutes every day for 30 days. During this time, comment on posts and connect with as many people as possible until the timer goes off. This is how you start a snowball effect.

Think "What's In It For Them?"

Create content that will be the most helpful to your audience and that they enjoy consuming like videos, podcasts, blogs, articles, and images.

Stick To Your Brand

Use the same fonts, colors, and logo everywhere you post so you are easily identifiable, your audience knows exactly how to find you, and they can relate to your brand.

CHAPTER THREE

9 WAYS TO BUILD AUTHORITY

What is building authority? Authority is a way to establish yourself as an expert in your field. You want to be the authority in your niche, your industry, your business, in whatever you are doing as an entrepreneur or small business owner. If you don't have authority in your business, then you don't really have a business. Authority is critical to having an online business that is operating effectively, the way it should be, and bringing you income.

1. CREATE AND COMMUNICATE WITH PASSION

Everything you create and communicate needs to come from a place of passion and excitement. Think about the big picture of why you are doing or saying something. Does it excite you? Do you convey that excitement to your audience? If not, work on it. You should love what you are doing and not get bored talking about it!

Anything you do in your business should stem from the desire to complete something, teach something, do something, show something, or share something. You should feel that knowledge, information, and excitement bubbling up inside you so much that it just needs to be shared with your audience.

For example: marketing. I love online marketing! It gets me excited. I get butterflies in my stomach when I am mapping out funnels for my clients and strategizing how we're going to bring them to their goal and objective, and planning in the ROI that they want to achieve. While I'm sitting there and planning that out, I get so excited for them because I see it, I see their vision.

Whatever your business is that you're passionate about, stand behind the product that you're selling or stand behind the idea that you are teaching and conveying.

You don't need to be salesy to convey that passion, either. The truth is, if you are the authority in your market and you can convey that, then people are going to want to work with you. No one wants to work with someone who doesn't feel passionate about what they're doing. People do want to work with business owners who seem knowledgeable and excited about their industry. The best way to demonstrate your passion and understanding is by providing value.

When you're able to give a lot of value around your topic, then people know that you are extremely knowledgeable, and they will want to work with you.

If you're selling health and wellness products, you should be passionate about having a healthy lifestyle, eating the right foods, sleeping well at night, and whatever else you define as health and wellness. If it's a healthy shake or a snack bar or some sort of product that you need to sell, you should be using that product and demonstrating the results. You're using the product, it's positively affecting and changing your body, your mindset, whatever it is, now you need to convey that to everybody else.

2. BE REAL

Another thing to do when building authority is to be genuine. Just be you. Talk like a real person, not a sales bot.

You want to be a real human, speaking as if you were talking to your best friend on the couch. How would you talk to them? You wouldn't be reading scripts. You wouldn't be going "Uh, was I supposed to say this or that first? I'm not really sure." Be genuine. Share what works, share what doesn't work. Speak from the heart.

You'll notice that I never say, "Buy my stuff! You have to buy my stuff! Sign up and be my client! You want me to run your ads for you!" I'm not doing that because that's salesy. That's just pitching without providing any passion, excitement, or value about my topic and that's no way to build a real relationship!

What you see me doing is talking about why you need Facebook ads and how running ads will help solve your problems. I'm talking to you about the difficulties that you're having in your business. I'm helping you strategize and think about different ways to do things in your business, so I'm really able to get a feel for what you need from me and I'm able to provide that for you. I'm providing value by helping you without any expectations in return.

If one day you say, "Gosh, I really wish someone could run ads for me," maybe you'll think of me because I've already provided a lot of value for you. I'll be on your mind because you've seen my Lives, or read my blog, or listened to my podcast so you're already aware that I know my stuff.

You're not going out into the world and saying, "Buy my stuff. Buy it. Buy it." Instead, you need to be saying, "Look how this has changed my life and I would love to be able to change your life as well."

Also, when you make a mistake, own it!

The other day I sent out an email to around 700 people and ended it the way I sign a lot of my emails, 'All the best, Meliss.' Well, I was copying one email of mine to the other email and then erasing as I go to make sure I have the same signature at the end. It said, "All the best", but the A and the L were erased, so it was just left with a lowercase "l" followed by "the best". So, it looked like I signed the email with 'I the best.'

"I the best."

Yikes.

Yes, that was a big mistake, but then I popped on a Facebook live and I let everyone know about it. I'm a human being and I want my followers to know! We all make mistakes. No fake stuff happening over here, what you see is what you get. It is so important because it's easy to lose that communication, that relationship-building with all the technology we have. But building those relationships is how you build your business.

People are not going to come to your door and say, "I can't wait to give you my money," unless you've built some sort of relationship with them. One where they know they can trust you, they know they need you, that you can help them, and that you're the one they want to take them to that next level.

When you go to buy something from somebody, a small business let's say, are you going to just do 'eenie meenie minie mo"? Or are you going to buy from somebody that's invested their time with you, taught you things, spoke to you, answered your questions, helped you out, made you feel

comfortable, maybe made you laugh? The people you build a
relationship with are the ones that are going to continue doing things with
you, including buying your services.

3. FIND A NICHE

First, decide what makes you special. Do you love to work with a certain
type of dog, moms who just had a baby, or business owners who manage
teams of 10 or more? What specific area can you specialize in?

You will communicate better with your ideal market and you will fine-tune
your skills particular to that industry if you choose to find a highly-specific
niche. People who need what you specialize in will see you as the
authority.

In a world of people who are doing the exact same you are, how are you
different? How can you stand out? How can you really show that you are
a special version of what everybody else is doing?

There're millions of virtual assistants, right? If you're a VA, you're going
to want to find a niche that you can specialize in so anyone looking for a
VA will see you as an expert. For example, are you a VA that helps
people in the health and wellness industry? That's a niche. Are you a VA
that helps stay at home moms? That's a niche. Are you a VA that helps
high-level executive business men and women book their travel and deal
with their schedule? That's a niche. Find a niche that you are good at,
that you have a passion for, and that can set you apart from the other
people who do what you do.

Once you find your niche, your unique intersection of skills and interests,
this is what happens: you become the authority in that niche. If there are a
million VAs and you're a specialized VA, then everyone that deals with
that specialty isn't going to go to all these other VAs, they're going to go to
you.

80% of my business is running marketing for the health and wellness
industry. Now, I know that someone who needs marketing in the health
and wellness industry is going to come to me, not go to someone who does
marketing for the music industry.

You want to be super niched because it helps you create that authority and, when you're working in the same field repeatedly, you'll get really good at it. You're getting practice at it and eventually you are going to be the best at it; better than anyone else could be. Then it'll be easier for you to replicate your systems. It will become easier and easier, and your skills will continue to increase.

4. BUILD SOCIAL PROOF

Social proof is so important in your business. Think about all the times you have wanted to go to a restaurant that you had never tried before, so you scrolled through Yelp or Yellow Pages and you checked out the reviews. If it had a one-star review, did you end up going? Probably not.

Think about online digital products that you've purchased. Have you ever purchased one that has zero testimonials? Probably not. It's very important that you have testimonials on your Facebook page and on your website. I always tell everyone, "you need to sprinkle your testimonials on every single page of your website, not just on the testimonial page." You want people to purchase things from you. The way that they know they can like and trust you right off the bat is seeing that other people have liked and trusted you before. I have five-star reviews and when people ask me for a reference, I tell them to go look at the reviews on LinkedIn, on Facebook, and on my website. I also send them a link to many of my testimonials.

If you don't have any testimonials, go out and get them. You can get them from people who are close to you, who can speak on your personality. If you're always punctual and/or you're trustworthy, those things are important. You can go to past clients and customers and ask them for a testimonial when you're done working with them, or even while you're working with them. Maybe they've sent you an email that says something nice— you can take a little snippet of that. You can ask employers, co-workers, people on your team to speak about your qualities so when new leads are ready to purchase from you, it's already there. Video testimonials are an excellent form of social proof.

Also, if you're just starting out, another great way to get some testimonials and social proof is to ask for it in groups. For example, in my group, Magnetic Marketing Mastermind, we do Trading Tuesdays. You can say, "Hey, I can make a free logo in exchange for a testimonial." Boom— you have a testimonial, they've got their logo. If they really love their logo, they're going to want to recommend you to other people through word of mouth.

Another thing that's great social proof is an industry quote that gets organically shared. If you have ever said anything that pertains to your industry and you think to yourself, "*That was pretty good shit I just said.*" Write it down, turn it into an image, post it, make sure that it's known that you said it, and brand it. You want to make sure that you're sharing those quotes so other people can see them and say, "Wow! That is a great hack." Or "I love that quote! Who said that? Oh, Meliss from Meliss Marketing did. She really knows her shit!"

Building authority is all about having people come back to you from all these different avenues online. That means that when somebody needs your services they know to go to you. You're the expert, you have built that authority because no matter where they are online they see you and they come right back to you, your Facebook page, your website, your sales funnel, whatever it is.

5. CONSISTENCY

You have got to be consistent because that's what building authority is all about.

Let's talk about Tony Robbins. Tony Robbins is a famous life coach and business coach. He owns 33 companies and every day he has the same routine. He lives his life in such a way that speaks to what he does. He's motivating. He's positive. He's consistent. You believe in him, you know that he's a great, famous person. He's helped other famous people achieve great things. It's not like he's this great, highly motivational speaker one day and then he doesn't post anything, doesn't do anything, stops touring the country, stops touring the world and just falls off the map for two months and then everyone's asking, "Where did Tony Robbins go? Who is he? Oh, we forgot about him." No! He's an authority because he shows up every single day. We rely on him being there every single day, same with Oprah, same with any influencer you resonate with.

Those people in your industry that are leading the way, show up every single day. They don't just disappear, they're in everybody's face all the time (in a good way). When you're showing up in everyone's newsfeeds with valuable content all the time, people know that they can trust you; that you're going to be there for them. They know that your next live stream is coming out on Tuesday. They know that they're going to get two emails from you every week. Whatever it is that you do, be consistent because that's how you're going to build your authority.

The people that are consistent are also the people that show up even when they don't want to. There are Tuesdays when I think, "*I want to stay in bed today. I don't feel like going live in four of my groups today.*" But I do it anyway, because I want to show up as the authority, I want to be consistent and I want people to know I'm here and I'm not going anywhere. If something comes up and I can't make it, I let my audience know. I don't just disappear.

Whatever your industry is, you need to do the same thing. Whatever consistency means to you, whether it's writing a blog once a week, doing two Facebook lives a week, releasing a YouTube video every week; whatever it is, show up and keep showing up.

Consistency also creates a momentum that continues to grow, snowballing its way into your successful lap. When the momentum is being built, consistency prevents it from crumbling. Automation is a great way to help keep your overwhelm at bay. You don't have to be everywhere at once, you just need to plan and execute... consistently.

6. CONTENT STRATEGY

This is so important in your business. If you do not have a content strategy, then your online business is already failing. It's true. You need to know what you're going to be talking about. What are you producing? What content are you creating? What content are you curating? Do you know the difference between create and curate?

Content strategy is the only way that you're going to be seen as a business and not as a hobby or just some fluff on the internet. There are so many things on the internet. You need to stand out and you can't do that without a plan, a strategy. You need to be able to say, "This week we are talking about building authority." Then, every single thing you do that week needs to relate to building authority. That's just one example, having a weekly theme, that's helpful to your content strategy.

Let's talk about the difference between content creation and content curation.

Creation of your content is where you actually create content: the images, the blogs, the podcast, the videos, all the information that you're producing, the PDFs, the emails, etc. All of that is content creation. You're making it. You're putting something new out into the world that is of use to people.

Let's say you're a finance coach. Creating content for a finance coach might look like creating blogs about how to go on a financial diet or producing a podcast that provides simple tips people can use to pay down their credit card debt or filming a video where you explain different types of loans and their benefits.

Curation is kind of like when you're in an art gallery and you have an art curator. They're the ones that decide which paintings are going in the gallery or which pieces are going to be accepted into the museum. They're choosing carefully, determining what is most important for the audience.

Let's say you don't have a lot of your own content right now, but you want to still be able to engage with your audience. You're going to choose content from other influencers in your industry that have good information that you stand behind and would be useful to your followers. So instead of creating new content you'll say, "Hey, look at this guy's content. He has amazing info that you will enjoy."

Let's go back to that financial coach example. If you're that financial coach, you might see an amazing article by Forbes or Bloomberg that you know will be of immense value to your followers. If you're curating your content, whether that's your Facebook business page or your Instagram account, you can share that article with some information about why you shared it. You could post a link on Facebook for your followers and say something like, "This article has an excellent tip about what to do when you get a fraudulent charge on your credit card!" Or "Watch this video by my fellow blogger about how to negotiate a better interest rate."

Curating shows your followers that you are committed to providing them with the best, most complete, and most updated information that will help them— even if it's not something you've made yourself. By speaking to what you found most helpful about the curated content, it also establishes your expertise for sorting out the good advice from the bad.

In your content strategy, you'll have creation and curation together. You can't possibly create new content daily on your own, it's not sustainable. So, plan to curate some useful pieces each day or each week that your followers can use.

7. PAID AND ORGANIC REACH

If you have high-quality content, that's what is going to reach your audience; that's what your audience is going to like and share and comment on. When they share it, it's going to travel and reach people organically, meaning without ad spend. They share it on their feed, someone else shares it onto their feed and before you know it, it's viral.

Paid reach is when you spend money on Facebook ads and, especially with the new Facebook algorithm, you need to have paid reach in order to reach all the leads and audiences you want to connect with.

You need to put some ad spend behind the posts that you want people to see, even your followers. This is going to position you as the authority because pushing ad spend behind your content will put your content in front of the exact people whom you want to see it, and Facebook is the most highly targeted platform.

If you're a dog walker and your niche is to walk dogs for the elderly, then in your Facebook advertising you can fine-tune the demographics you're targeting. The audience will have the right income, so they'll be able to afford your services, they're located where you do your dog walking, and they are a certain age bracket.

You can really break down who is in your niche and where you're putting your ads so that those people, your ideal target market, are the only ones who are going to see that ad. Because you are serving an ad to the people who want what you create, serve, or do in your niche, you become the authority. When they're scrolling their newsfeed, you are exactly the type

18

of business they're looking for and you're putting your ad directly in front of the people who you serve.

You become the niche in that it's almost like you're speaking to them, "Oh my gosh, you're talking to me. You're talking to me. I'm 75. I have a dog and I need someone to walk my dog and here's an ad for 75-year-old's who need their dog walked!"

You want to be able to know your niche and your target market so well that you are only paying to place your ad directly in front of the exact people that you want to see it; the people who are most likely to buy it. You're speaking to them. You become the authority because when they talk to their friends they say, "Oh my gosh, you wouldn't believe what I found! A dog walking service just for us!"

You automatically become the authority with this technique, so use paid reach to go along with your organic strategy.

8. CREATE A FOLLOWING

Another way to build authority and extend your reach is to create a following. This can be on or offline. You can do it in the networking groups at the Chamber of Commerce in your area, or online in Facebook or LinkedIn groups. I recommend you cultivate a following on your business page (here's some behind-the-scenes high-end Facebook strategy)... Utilize your business page and share it to your personal page to increase your reach.

Engage with your audience. When you're creating this following, people are getting to know you; they want to know about you, how you act, how you behave, what you sound like, and whether they like you.

Create this following of people who know you and like you and, of course, trust you. They trust that you're going to be there. They trust you're going to answer their questions. They trust that you know your stuff and that you are who you say you are, and that comes from building this following.

The best way to build a following is by providing value in the groups you create and other places online. In your group, that can be done a number of ways. You can provide a daily tip, do some live videos, and share other industry information.

For example, if you're a nutrition coach, you can start a Facebook group where you share healthy recipes, do live meal prep videos, and even link to your favorite workouts. All these steps position you as an authority. They show that you know what you're talking about and you're willing to put it up to the test of your audience. Those that follow you, whether that's in an online group or in real life, ask questions about your industry, and you need to be able to answer with the utmost confidence and competence.

You can also cultivate your following outside of those groups. When you are reading blogs of those in your industry, comment below them with some insight. Join LinkedIn groups, Facebook groups, Meet-ups, and comment below people's posts offering advice or information that will be helpful. Make it a point to add yourself to the conversation. Let people know what you do and show them how you can help them. These comments are searchable and live on forever so showcasing your expertise can eventually connect you wit others that are seeking advice on the topic.

9. BE A GUEST

Another way to establish authority is to be a guest on someone else's platform. You could do that through blog posts or podcasts. Someone could interview you for their podcast, or maybe you'll write a blog that you can guest blog for on somebody else's site. Maybe somebody's doing a summit and you could be one of the people on the summit, or if there's a webinar maybe you're the special guest. Any time you can do something like that, where you cross over into somebody else's arena, it is really beneficial for boosting your authority and getting noticed by people in your niche.

When you guest blog on somebody else's blog, you're showing that you know information that the blogger's audience may benefit from— you're not going to have the same exact niche as the blogger, but you'll overlap. It's a bit like a Venn Diagram. Let's say you are a weight loss coach for moms who just had a baby. That's your circle, "weight loss coach for moms that just had a baby". Then there's another platform that belongs to someone who talks to stay-at-home moms about their experiences. Not everybody in your niche is going to be a stay-at-home mom, and not everybody in the stay-at-home mom blog just had a baby, but there is going to be overlap where you're providing value and information to previously untapped leads.

It often goes beyond overlap in just your niche. Using your podcast episode or your blog as a guest means that you're going to have access to people in the other circle that you didn't have access to before, so you're gaining authority in your niche and the outskirts of your niche. Guest blogging, speaking, or videos are all really powerful tools that you can use to establish that authority.

These strategies are what you need to do in order to have a booming online business, *business* being the keyword. Something that's generating money for you, not just a hobby or a side gig. If you really want a successful online business, you have to spend time working on building authority.

CHAPTER FOUR
CREATE YOUR CREDIBILITY

To create credibility, we need to focus on what your strengths are: If you aren't sure what those are, ask!

Think about those that are closest to you in family, friendship, and business, and pick 1 person from each category. Ask them what strengths they see in you.

You could also think about what excites you. What could you speak on for hours that makes you either speak quickly or with passion?

I want you to figure out what your zone of genius is. Where can you excel the most? What is something that you do differently than others or that makes you stand out?

Make a list of all these things and compile them into 1 list of your positive attributes. Then, I want you to make a story about yourself in your business using these adjectives as a way to incorporate the attributes into your business.

What My Family Says	What My Friends Say	What My Colleagues Say	What I Can Speak On For Hours	What I Can Do Differently To Stand Out

Author and life coach Barbara Sher shares an example of someone who is organized, creative, and friendly with a passion for baking. You can see the article on the next page.

How often have you gotten a compliment on your creativity or your patience or your resilience, only to wave it off, assuming that these strengths must come easily to everyone? In my 30 years as a lifestyle/career coach and author, the mistake I see people make time and again is failing to recognize their talents. An honest inventory may be difficult—even impossible—for you to do yourself. So sit with a friend and try this exercise. It's a new twist on something I call the Self-Correcting Life Scenario, and it's one of my favorites.

1. Ask your friend to name three of your strengths (The words in the image above may provide some inspiration.)

2. Tell your friend your top passion. Then have your friend tell an imaginary story of your life, based on this passion and your strengths. For instance, "You're organized, creative, and friendly, and your passion is baking. So, you run a bakery where customers can buy cupcakes with little icing portraits of themselves."

3. Take a minute to imagine this fantasy as your real life. Tell your friend what appeals to you ("Making cupcakes with artistic frosting would be awesome!") and what makes you cringe ("I'd never start my own business—the thought of bookkeeping gives me hives").

4. Now your friend revises the story based on your feedback. ("Okay, you organize monthly bake sales at the local Boys & Girls Club. Kids buy the cupcakes and paint their own portraits.")

5. Keep going back and forth until the story feels right. This may take three or 13 rounds—there's no need to rush. Your friend will likely suggest unexpected scenarios. Don't let knee-jerk objections ("That would cost too much!" "When would I have time?") shape your feedback. This is about crafting a scenario tailored to your strengths.

6. Stop when the story feels completely satisfying. You've just shaped your passion into a goal and defined what you do and don't want from your calling.

(Higher quality images can be found at HashtagExpertBook.com/resources)

Start with 10 strengths and decide which of those you are most passionate.

Narrow the list down until you have 3-5.

Then, go into Facebook and in the search bar, put in a key word to your industry. If you are in the fitness field, maybe you'll put the word "fitness" or if you are in wellness, you could put "wellness" in the box. That's going to bring up categories of things that relate to that word like posts, groups, pages, videos, events, etc.

Go into these groups and read these posts and comment on them. Start surveying the market to see if there is a need for your passion. Test the market and phrase your posts in such a way that will get people to be interested and answer you. Open-ended questions work best. Do this separately for each one of those passions.

You can also do this by going into groups that you are already a part of in your industry and use the search bar within the group to search for keywords that will bring up past posts and discussions.

The thing is, if you create content that speaks directly to the people in your market when you know there is a need for it, you will be hitting a gold mine. So, you are going to combine your strengths and passions with the market need and that's how you achieve success. Your target market is going to feel like you are speaking directly to them in the language that they use, and they will just want more and more from you!

Join email lists of the top 2 influencers in your industry that you really look up to. These are the people you are aspiring to be, so surround yourself with these people because they are where you want to go. Take note on what they are doing. Which groups are they a part of? How are they connecting with their audience? I don't want you to stalk them or steal their stuff, I just want you to put your research goggles on and pay close attention to these few people that you feel are doing an amazing job within your industry.

I tell you to limit it to 2 because it can become very overwhelming; your inbox will quickly be inundated with emails if you join any more than that.

We already discussed the know, like, and trust factor but this is particularly true when it comes to creating credibility.

When you are first starting out, offer your services in exchange for referrals. Help people in the industry in exchange for testimonials. Social proof is a huge factor in credibility. People want to know what others think and feel before they take their own chance.

You can give away free consultation calls or you can answer people's questions in the community. Do whatever you can to build relationships and add value. This will create the credibility you want and need. Then, you'll start to see that you will get paying clients because people love the value you provide and they'll come ready to take action.

Give more value!! Create a lead magnet that resonates with 1 problem your audience has that you can solve. Giving away free, valuable information will create your credibility and help nurture your prospects. There will be a time for selling but it's too early in the game. You must go through the nurture process before the selling process. When you do this, your sales will have a higher conversion.

So, when you ask questions, the answers you receive are extremely valuable. You are literally getting an insider-look as to what your prospects top pain points are that they are dealing with. The strategy lies in the fact that you can be reaching out and providing value way before you have an opt-in, so build your momentum and keep asking questions. Offer lots of free value in your market while you create something behind the scenes to offer them that specifically solves the problems you are helping them with.

It's genius! And it's how you get your prospects to trust you and join your list. You get them, they get you, and the relationship begins.

CHAPTER FIVE
THE ONE THING EVERY BIZ NEEDS

There is one thing that every business needs that they can't do for themselves: **social proof.**

Social proof is a social/psychological phenomenon where people adopt the actions or opinions of others they trust. It's all the things you have online that show you're legitimate, worthy, and will help others make the decision to buy from you.

So why does this matter for your business?

You can use the underlying concepts behind social proof to market your business! Social proof is more powerful than any marketing campaign. Let's explore the different types of social proof.

Reviews are the most common type of social proof.

Just last week I was shopping on Amazon for a face wash. I came across one that had 2,607 reviews and 4.5 stars. *Of course* I bought it. That many people can't possibly be wrong! No matter what kind of business you have, reviews are the backbone of your social proof.

Some sellers provide incentives for reviews, whether they are positive or negative, because they know how important they are.

You can do the same for your business. Follow up with customers and offer a discount on future services or purchases if they are willing to write you a review on social media. To keep things ethical, be sure to remind them that you want their *honest* opinion and that you aren't asking for positive reviews only.

That said, if you come across some negative reviews, respond to them in a polite manner. It's always a good idea to touch base with unhappy customers to see if you can repair the relationship and regain their trust.

This is the first thing you should work on.

Reviews show others that you are a functioning business and give them confidence to purchase from you. No one wants to be the first or the guinea pig, they'd prefer to buy from a reputable business and know they're getting what they paid for. Don't wait until something goes badly and end up with negative reviews. Ask for it! There is no shame in asking someone to rate your business or leave a review. In fact, I'd encourage you to have a follow-up system in place for acquiring reviews after the sale is complete.

Recommendations from friends are the most powerful form of social proof. According to a Nielsen report from Sep. 2015, 83% of consumers in 60 countries say that they trust recommendations from family and friends more than any other type of advertising. Friends typically share similar locations, budgets, and interests so their suggestions may seem more attainable.

Referrals are an excellent way to attract new customers. We have a tendency to trust our friends and acquaintances and if they are giving you a recommendation through word-of-mouth; that's gold! Your customer service can and will make or break your opportunity for referrals. People remember how they are treated and especially remember how you made them feel. If you go above and beyond and make someone feel exceptional, they will remember that and be more than willing to openly share their experience. If you've done your work, you should have no qualms about reaching out periodically and asking for referrals. Always ask new customers how they heard about you and if someone refers you, always show appreciation and gratitude for that. Let them know how much you value their business and the referral.

Testimonials provide valuable details to your customers.

Sometimes, even a client doesn't know what they want. I recently made the decision to cut my hair, which I've been growing out for *ages*. When the time came to cut and donate my hair, I started reading reviews for local salons. Yes, the stars were a good indicator of quality, but they didn't tell me much about the stylists. Then I came upon a review that described a stylist as "fun to talk to, willing to go slowly and listen to what I wanted, and she even taught me how to style my new haircut." Yes! That's exactly what I needed— which I wouldn't have known without the passionate testimonial.

Depending on your type of business, you can reach out directly to clients to request a testimonial, or you can feature positive reviews as testimonials on your website or business page. The best testimonials come from strong relationships, so only ask for a testimonial if you have a stellar client relationship.

Another type of testimonial that's becoming increasingly common is the real-time purchase pop-up. You may have seen this on some e-commerce websites. It's a simple plug-in on websites that shows a short statement and a link, like "Sarah from Indiana just bought our *Into the Woods* khaki jacket!"

Written testimonials and quotes from customers are an excellent choice for adding to your website or using as posts on social media. When someone gives you encouraging words or great feedback, shout it to the rooftops (always get permission first). You earned the praise; don't be afraid to show it off.

You'll get huge bonus points if you can get a video testimonial. Seeing someone else talk about you and your business will do more for your marketing than most print services. One way to get these testimonials is to offer clients something in return. A free product, service, discount or gift of gratitude will go a long way. If they're happy with what you've done for them, they'll be glad to do it.

Endorsements work best on social media. If you have an expert, influencer, or author within your network or industry, work hard to build a relationship with them and take advantage of any opportunity for them to try out what you have to offer. Getting a celebrity to praise or promote your product automatically gives you appeal and credibility. Their network is a huge market you wouldn't normally be able to tap into. Identify who these people are in your community and get connected with them right away.

Experts can also provide social proof. How many times have you seen the phrase "9 out of 10 dentists agree!" or "Certified Organic" on packages? Expert endorsements are both *expected* and *essential* for certain types of products and services.

Celebrities frequently pitch every product you can imagine. Skin care? ✓ Hair products? ✓ Clothing, makeup, vitamins? ✓ ✓ ✓ There's a reason that brands give their products to celebrities and pay them for endorsements: *it works!* Everyone wants to be a little more like their favorite celeb and, since we can't all afford personal trainers and stylists, sometimes we settle for using their favorite shampoo.

Influencers are becoming a common piece of social proof and marketing. Some Influencers have hundreds of thousands of followers while others might have just a few hundred. Either type can be powerfully influential based on their followers' engagement level.

Tons of businesses use influencer marketing to increase their social proof. On a small scale, this can be as simple as providing free products or services in exchange for an honest review or shoutout on social media.

Some bloggers have made this model their entire business, with their followers clamoring to scoop up products that they recommend. You can take advantage of this trend by collaborating with bloggers on sponsored posts or content.

On a larger scale, businesses pay www.influenster.com and www.bzzagent.com to send their products to highly-targeted groups of testers who will review the products online.

Social Media shares can have a positive or negative impact on your business, depending on the reason for the share. If you're going viral, make sure it's for a hilarious marketing campaign and not for a major customer service issue.

Actual Proof is vital for small businesses that are just starting out before they acquire a large following and social status. If that sounds like you, think about creating a portfolio of work, examples of other businesses who have used your services, or awards you have won, and add them to your website or business page."

If you're just getting started in business or you want to work on developing a stronger online presence, you need Social Proof. This is a key element to your online reputation and will be critical for your growth.

More people are using apps and social media to look up companies, services and products and what they find will determine whether or not they will buy. Social Proof is highly important for growth and if you don't have it, you need to make it a priority to get it.

Your Number will speak for itself if your following is big enough. People are more apt to purchase from someone who has 10,000 fans as opposed to someone who has 21. I've never been a fan of chasing likes but with a large enough following, in the right online space, you can set yourself apart from the competition.

The best way to make social media work for you is to have a solid social media strategy that connects you with your potential customers and to have processes in place that consider all the elements of social proof.

Social Proof is about getting people to know you, like you, trust you and ultimately, purchase from you.

By the way, if you liked this chapter, you'll LOVE my juicy Free Guide I published on how to stop stressing out about getting in front of your best customer. It's titled "Finding Your Dream Customer" Guide. Download all resources at www.HashtagExpertBook.com/resources

CHAPTER SIX

CAN YOU GET ME A KLEENEX PLEASE?

Imagine your brand being so well-known that it becomes a catch-all term for a specific product or service. That's the kind of brand awareness that companies like Kleenex, Google, and Band-Aid have achieved.

I mean, how often have you heard phrases like these?

"Could you get me a Kleenex, please?"

"Go Google it!"

"Ouch! Do you need a Band-Aid?"

On the opposite end of the spectrum, we have brand slogans that are so well-known, they stand in for the brand names themselves.

Let's play a quick game: how fast can you name the companies based on their catchphrase or slogan?

Just Do It.

I'm lovin' it.

Melts in your mouth, not in your hands.

Yeah, those are Nike, McDonald's, and M&Ms . What's amazing about these companies is that they are so well-known we can recognize them from slogans alone. And, let's be real, these slogans aren't exceptional by themselves— they require that brand awareness to have this effect.

SO, WHAT IS BRAND AWARENESS?

It's the extent to which customers are aware of a brand. Simple, right? How well do your customers know your brand? Are they familiar with your brand values? What about the distinctive qualities that set you apart from other companies with similar products or services?

Brand awareness is what takes a brand from *"Who?"* to *"Who else would I choose?"*

Let's look at two examples:

Google, which was founded in 1998, and Band-Aid bandages, which began way back in 1920. Both brand names are synonymous with the service or product they provide. Google, a much newer company by all accounts, was able to exponentially increase their brand awareness through innovative marketing techniques. Band-Aid has been around forever, providing quality products and appealing directly to their target market.

Maybe you're saying, "Sure, Meliss. That sounds great, but we can't all be Google or Band-Aid!"

Well, I am saying, "Why not try?"

Sure, you might not have the type of business that can be scaled to that sort of massive, worldwide level. But there's no reason why you can't be the Google of wherever you're from.

You can be the go-to in your industry... And it all starts with brand awareness.

Here are 4 steps you can take to improve your brand awareness.

1. BE A HUMAN

Customers don't want to talk to a brand or an idea, they want to talk to humans. That's why it's **so** important to determine your brand persona. Figure out your unique selling proposition, brand values, the type of personality and voice your brand will use, and how your brand will show up in real life. *Then stick to it.* Be consistent with your voice and your message so that your customers know what to expect every time they interact with you.

2. SOCIALIZE

Once you know who *you* are, figure out who your ideal customer is. Then, go where they are. Whether that's on social media or real-life events— get in front of your customers! If your ideal customer is an Instagram-obsessed #girlmom, then you should post regularly on Instagram, use the same hashtags she's using, and interact with other accounts she likes. If your ideal customer is a business-savvy LinkedIn user?

Yep. You guessed it. Start posting on LinkedIn!

Pay attention to the type of content that your customers are engaging with on these platforms. Do they lean towards emotionally-driven pieces or are they sharing the latest iteration of a popular meme?

3. TALK THE TALK

Now that you're on the right platforms and interacting and engaging with your targets, pay close attention to the way they talk, both to you and about you. What sort of language and phrases are they using? What questions are they asking about your brand? What problems do they have that you can solve?

Incorporating this language into your social media posts and your other content, like emails and blog posts, will show your customers that you understand them. Grab my "30 Content Ideas To Kill It On Social Media".

Download all my resources at www.HashtagExpertBook.com/resources

4. TELL A STORY

Remember back at step number one, where I told you to be a human? That's a big thing right here. People connect to relatable narratives, so tell a story! You can go deep and emotional, like American Greetings did with their *insanely viral* Mother's Day campaign (search #worldstoughestjob), hilarious like the time Fruit of the Loom asked men to #PutAShirtOn, or completely unique like the time Ikea encouraged people to pee on their advertisement. Each of these examples are highly relatable, highly shareable content that consumers went crazy for.

The type of content you share, the way you say it, and where you're sharing it are all determined by the previous steps.

Now, go put this information to work! Even if you don't have your brand persona completely nailed down, you can start doing market research. Learn where your customers are and start engaging with them there. This can help inform the type of brand you want to be and how you want to show your personality.

Want to learn how to use these strategies to up level your business?

Check out my Social Marketing Academy at
www.HashtagExpertBook.com/resources

CHAPTER SEVEN

REMEMBER ZACK MORRIS

Any other Saved by the Bell fans? We're going to do one of those Zack Morris flashbacks to a few years ago...

I was a single mom on food stamps. I had three jobs, but I couldn't pay the rent while also juggling the roles of mom, dad, maid, chauffeur, and chef.

I was burnt out, broken down, and unable to make ends meet.

While learning how to market one of my businesses, I discovered Facebook ads. Some of my fellow entrepreneur friends saw what I was doing, and they asked me to run their ads as well.

I kept learning, signed up for training courses, and hired a business coach. Slowly, very slowly, I built a business and started to make some money.

Success.

Finally.

But, life gets in the way.

My children's dad came back into town and decided to sue for custody. Suddenly, I was dragged back down into debt through lawyer fees. I was back at square one, but that didn't stop me.

I kept showing up. I didn't quit, and I definitely didn't let a little failure stop me.

So, why am I telling you all this?

This is my story. This is my *why*. Not just why I do what I do, but also why my clients choose me. When they speak to me, they hear my story, and they learn the most important thing about me: I put in the work.

You have stories, too. Those stories are an essential part of your business, and it's important to tell them. Our stories do more than make us who we are, they help us connect on a meaningful level with prospects.

Let's dig a bit to help you find your story.

Recently, I watched a great TEDx Talk by JP Sears about saying YES to weirdness. It made me realize: you're probably not weird enough.

So how do you find your story?

Just be weirder.

Leads won't want to work with you just because they like your business name, or your great branding, or your well-written Facebook ads. Those things will bring them to you, but it's your YOU-ness (that's a word now) that will convince them to work with you.

That's why you have to be weird. Own the parts of you that make you uncomfortable. Be brave enough to be different. Be unapologetically YOU.

The big idea behind USPs (unique selling point) is that every business has something that makes them stand out. Yours is easier to find than you think.

Talk to your favorite clients or best customers and ask them why they chose to work with you.

Maybe they liked your attention to detail, or your sense of humor, or the way you accomplish tasks way ahead of time. Take that thing that sets you apart and get weird with it.

Don't just be attentive to detail, be obsessive about it. Show off that unique sense of humor. Think of stories about yourself that highlight these details and embrace them!

CHAPTER EIGHT

HOW TO DISCOVER YOUR DREAM CLIENT AND WHY IT'S IMPORTANT IN YOUR BUSINESS

In the digital space, it's common for me to see posts and talk to business owners about how to find customers; usually because what they're doing now isn't working.

More often than not, it isn't their efforts holding them back. Instead, it's not reaching the right people at the right time.

You see, in order to achieve growth with loyal clients and repeat business it's important to understand completely who your ideal customer is. Once you're able to nail down who precisely needs what you have to offer and is willing to pay for it, you'll be able to find them, sell to them, and satisfy their needs.

It's unlikely you're a one-stop shop that has something that everyone wants; because of that, you need to do the work and find out who it is that's going to pay you for what you have to offer.

No more advertising to large volumes of people hoping to get lucky with a sale. Instead, your advertising is going to a targeted group and is written especially for them. It's intentional.

If you know who your ideal client is then all sales efforts, advertising, and marketing has a clear focus for gaining new business.

If you're ready to take your business to the next level and willing to do your homework, read on.... Here's how you, too, can discover who your ideal client is.

Know Your Business From The Customer's Perspective:

Since we own the business, we assume we know everything about it... wrong! We often see things from the owner's view instead of a customer's point of view.

Grab a pen and paper and start by writing down precisely what you offer to your customers. This isn't your product, it's what your product does for them (this might be harder than you think). You'll want to identify what problem you're solving for them and who would find value in what you're offering. Once you've done that, consider the competition and ask yourself how you compare (be honest) and what makes you stand out from them. You might discover you have a little work to do.

Let's recap, you're asking yourself these questions:

- What am I offering and what does it do for my customer?
- What problem am I solving?
- Who would find value in what I have to offer?
- How do I stack up to the competition? What sets me apart?

Build A Customer Profile:

Now that you've done the research and have a glimpse into whom your ideal client might be, it's time to build a customer profile. Think of the customer profile as a detailed description of who they are and what makes them tick. Interviewing past and prospective clients is a great way to uncover:

- Your customer's demographics – age, gender, income etc.
- Personality type and preferences
- Behavior – their likes and dislikes, hobbies, etc.
- Location – where they live or spend the most time
- Online habits – where they hang out, what they are reading and what they are searching for

Create Your Client Avatar:

Now that you've laid the foundation and done your homework, you're ready for the most important part of all; creating your client avatar. Being able to present your talents, products and services to your precise customer is critical in gaining new business. Think of your avatar as a fictional, yet life-like, representation of who your customer is.

Taking this highly important step and creating an avatar that represents your ideal client will guide you through current and future business decisions as you decide what solutions you will offer, which products to sell and who to target in your marketing efforts.

To simplify this process for you, I've created a FREE Finding Your
Dream Customer Guide to aide you in discovering your dream client and
creating your very own avatar.

I can't reiterate enough how important it is to know your ideal client inside
and out. Knowing who you need to make a connection with, who you
need to help, and who to sell to IS the essence to a successful business.

Don't forget to download my very valuable and useful Finding Your
Dream Customer Guide.

Download all resources at www.HashtagExpertBook.com/resources

CHAPTER NINE
WHY YOU SHOULD BE A CONTROL FREAK

List building is an important way to grow your business.

But there is one major difference between social media marketing and email marketing: CONTROL!

On social media, you have control over who sees your targeted Facebook ads and things you post in groups. Besides that, those ever-changing algorithms on social media platforms can make it difficult for the right prospects to see your organic content.

Email marketing is different.

Your email list is the only place you will find a group of people who are

A) Already invested in you

B) Only able to see exactly what you want them to see

How amazing is that?

That level of control is HUGE. You have the power to give your list great insights, make them laugh, and gently guide them to the outcome you both want: a relationship.

You want a client, they want some help.

It's a match made in heaven and it builds your authority!

Which is why you must be very careful with the list.

I follow thousands of people on social media! Only a very small fraction of them are lucky enough to get my email.

When a prospect joins your list, what they're really doing is allowing you to enter their digital home: their inbox. And if there is one thing we all hate, it's junk mail.

**The best thing you can do to build and maintain your email list is
to give your subscribers the high-quality content they deserve.**

Not another advertisement for a service they aren't even sure they
need.

Over in my Social Marketing Academy, I teach about list building.
You'll learn how to get them to opt-in, how to build trust to convert
prospects into paying clients, and my top five tips for email marketing.

Download all resources at www.HashtagExpertBook.com/resources

CHAPTER TEN

STAND UP TO STAND OUT

By now, we all know we need a Unique Selling Proposition (USP). Our USP helps us identify how we will stand out against a sea of entrepreneurs and online businesses. It's the thing we say when people ask us what we do.

What if there's another way? What if you didn't just stand out, but you stood up?

Imagine your business being known not just for what you do, but how you do it. You're not just a Facebook marketing specialist, you're the Facebook Marketing Guru who stands up for the empowerment of minority business owners.

See what a difference that makes?

Standing up for what you believe in helps you stand out even more.

When you're passionate about a subject, that fervor is infused in everything you do. Your eyes sparkle, your words shine, and your excitement is contagious. When you stand up for something that transforms you, you become more than just a business owner. You become a leader.

The old-school way of thinking was that we have to appeal to a wide demographic.

The new-school way of thinking is to have a very specific niche. So specific that your beliefs might even alienate a few people, and that's exactly what you want to do.

Your niche is your network. It's the group of people that you are speaking to directly. But even the most narrow niches have a lot of competition.

How do you stand out?

By standing up.

Picture it this way:

You're fishing in a lake. You could throw out a net and hope to catch a couple of fish as they swim by. Or, you could narrow down your focus to a specific type of fish. Figure out what bait they like and cast your fishing line right where they are swimming. That's speaking to your niche.

Now imagine that you're not only fishing in the right spot with the right bait, but you've attached a special lure to your rod. That lure is sparkly, it's unique, and it catches their eye.

That lure is the thing you stand up for. It's the thing that people look at and say "Oh. I feel that way too."

What do you stand up for? What causes or topics are you passionate about, and how can you tie that into your business?

Here are a couple of examples:

A blogger who stands up for inclusivity by using gender-neutral language.

A photographer who stands up for body positivity by not airbrushing out stretch marks and cellulite.

A biz coach who supports veterans by promoting veteran small-biz owners.

Now, which business owner is going to get more press and attention? Yet another generic business coach or one of the one I described above?

CHAPTER ELEVEN
THE 4 THINGS YOU SHOULD BE DOING RIGHT NOW TO GET MORE CLIENTS

When you are just starting out online, you may find that getting clients is a **BIG** challenge.

If you are a coach or have an online business, you may be thinking...

How do I meet so many people that are my ideal client?

How do I connect with them?

How will I find them?

If you have a brick and mortar business but you're just starting to see the value of expanding your reach on social, you may be saying to yourself...

I'm just throwing away my money to FB ads.

I can't find people to purchase my services!

How will I sign my first client online?

But I have an affordable plan to help make others see you as the expert in your industry (and that's what it's all about online)!

Before spending money online (or while you are simultaneously running ads) do these 4 things...

1. GET VISIBLE ONLINE

By this I mean, put yourself out there! Get in front of everyone! You can do this by joining online groups and being active in them. Don't think about it too much, just throw yourself into the conversation.

Respond to comments that peak your interest or are speaking about something related to your industry (this is easier if you are in a group that has to do with the services you offer or that is filled with your dream customer).

The goal is to network and connect. I like to do this in Instagram direct message, Facebook private message, and of course, with LinkedIn. It's a great tool to get in touch with the people, coaches, and companies that need your products and services.

2. GET VISIBLE OFFLINE

Depending on your introverted or extroverted status, you may prefer one of these over the other. The truth is, if you want people to know that you and your offers exist, you gotta get in front of them! So, step outside of your comfort zone and take your networking-self offline too.

Join meetups and groups that center around businesses or entrepreneurship and attend any get-togethers that you can. Go to networking events for business owners. Tell those that you have served to spread the word about how they liked your service.

In order to grow, you need to reach as many people as possible and surrounding yourself with other business owners is a great way to stay relevant and part of the conversation. Even if those business owners don't need your product or service right now, they may need it later or know someone else who could benefit. The more often you are on their mind, the more likely they will recommend you.

3. CREATE GREAT, VALUABLE CONTENT AND BE CONSISTENT

Content marketing is a truly powerful way to show your audience that you are the expert in your field and you really know your stuff. When you are posting valuable content consistently, you are also showing them that you are reliable and you follow-through (both great business characteristics)!

When you are able to offer so much value to your audience for free, they will be so intrigued to find out what your paid content must look like.

Educate your audience and build their trust by always over-delivering. When the time comes and they need what you're offering, they will be turning to you for help.

4. CONTINUE GIVING VALUE AND DO IT AGAIN

I already mentioned above how you should over-deliver and be consistent but here's the thing, it's really, really, *really* important. The second you slack on offering value, the next person or business will come swinging in and claim your space. Stay consistent. Provide tons and tons of value and then even if you don't feel like it, do it again!

If you are struggling with content creation, my free guide will help you. It's called my "30 Days Of Content Ideas To Kill It On Social Media".

Download all resources at www.HashtagExpertBook.com/resources

CHAPTER TWELVE

HOW TO GO VIRAL EVEN IF YOU CAN'T YODEL

Tell me what these things have in common:

- Laurel vs. Yanni

- Walmart Yodeling Kid

- THE DRESS

- "Leave Britney Alone"

- "David After Dentist"

- "Charlie Bit My Finger"

If you said, "Meliss, you spend way too much time watching and sharing them," you're right. Blunt, but right (also, how did you know?!)

Anyway, those are all examples of content that went crazy viral.

That's what we're talking about in this chapter.

To get you started, check out this infographic by Outgrow:

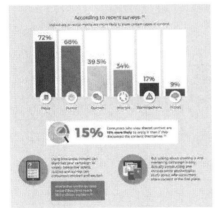

(Higher quality images can be found at HashtagExpertBook.com/resources)

I'll give you the highlights:

• News, humor, and opinion are the top three topics that go viral.

• Two psychological phenomena, novelty and information gap theory, are useful tools for creating content that has the potential to go viral.

• Positive emotions are way more effective for driving viral content.

• The top ten reasons people share content are to:

1- Connect with someone over a shared interest

2- Promote a product they believe is useful

3- Be involved in a current trend

4- Be the first to tell a friend about an event

5- Share something about themselves

6- Socialize with friends offline

7- Promote a good cause

8- Demonstrate their own knowledge on a subject

9- Start an online conversation

10- Gain opinions of friends

So, why are we discussing this?

Well, two reasons: a piece of content that goes viral can bring in major business and, if you're not quite able to go viral, you can still use this knowledge to make content that resonates.

Whenever I create content for my business, I ask myself some questions.

- Will <<*You, the one reading this right now*>> like this?

- Will <<*You, the one reading this right now*>> find it useful?

- Will <<*You, the one reading this right now*>> talk to someone about this piece of content?

And yes, I'm being totally serious! My followers are the best people to keep in mind while I'm creating. Everything I write is intended to be interesting and useful for you.

To build authority online, I want you to think like this too.

CHAPTER THIRTEEN
ARE YOU HIDING BEHIND YOUR BUSINESS

The other day I was running ads for a client and we created one ad that had conversational text and another ad using the exact same language but in video format. The video ad outdid the text ad by 60%.

Unfortunately, many entrepreneurs are still not using video in their marketing and it shows...

Users are more likely to engage with your video content over any other content out there. That alone should nudge you to create video content for your users.

Now, you may be thinking...

"I don't know what to say."

"I don't like the way I look/sound on video."

"What if nobody shows up for my lives?"

"I feel so awkward on camera."

But here's the thing...

Your competitors are using video and you need to be doing what your competitors are doing. PLUS, video builds authority.

Your peeps are asking for more video content and you need to be providing your users with what they need.

Facebook actually rewards those that use video on their platform. This means that if you don't use video, your content is not going to show up as often in the news feed as it could.

Here are a few ideas of how you can effectively use video content:

1. SAY THANKS!

A great way to start out on video is to thank your customers. You can make the customer feel special, let them know that you listen to their suggestions, and serve as a small pitch for your services. A great smile can go a long way on this one, too.

The great news is that if you are uncomfortable going live, you can pre-record this one and use it as a Facebook ad to target your market, embed it in an email, or post it on your wall.

2. SHARE CUSTOMER STORIES

Stories make people feel something: happy, sad, angry, excited, frustrated... and when you can get your prospects to use their emotions, they immediately connect better with your brand.

Sharing a story that happened to a customer, like a before/after, is a great way to connect to your ideal client, educate your audience of the transformation and success they can achieve from your product/service, and offer social proof.

3. PULL BACK THE CURTAIN

A great way to use video is to take your customers behind the scenes. This really helps your audience understand your unique personality and brand message. It's also a fun way to get your audience to engage. Instagram and Facebook stories are a great example of this.

If the only hesitation you have with video is fear, let me remind you, that negative thinking will not overcome fear, but action will. We get better when we try things, so don't judge yourself and just do it! After you've got that 1st video under your belt, you'll be on your way to many more video successes and you will see a boost in your engagement.

CHAPTER FOURTEEN
WHY YOU SHOULD BE MAPPING OUT YOUR WINS

If you've been following me for a while, you'll know I am all about positivity.

My glass isn't just half-full, it's overflowing!

One of the reasons I'm so positive is that I work for it. I take time each day to reflect on the good things that have happened, and what I'm looking forward to next.

I'm telling you this because it's had a major impact on my business.

Running a business is a lot of work, but it can also be a lot of fun! One of the best ways to bring in more positivity is to map out your wins.

Here's what that looks like:

Open up your spiral notebook, journal, Word document, or that scrap of paper you keep on your desk.

Think back to when you first started your business, whether that was 10 days or 10 years ago.

Now, think of all your wins. Start with the smallest win you can think of. Was it making your first dollar? Was it quitting your day job? Write that first one down, and then the next, and the one after that— all the way up to today.

Keep it going! Track your wins on a daily or weekly basis, no matter how small.

If you've been in the game a while, take a moment to notice something... Those small accomplishments have added up, haven't they?

Or, if you're still in the beginning of your journey, get pumped! Those small wins are going to stack up to something major.

Now that you've made your list, you might be wondering... Okay, but why?

Those wins aren't just a list of accomplishments to look at to get warm, fuzzy feelings. Those wins are the evidence of your hard work and success. Those wins shout out to the world "Look what I have accomplished!"

Here's a little secret: it's totally cool to brag about your accomplishments from time to time. You worked hard for them!

Look at your list and notice how small wins (like gaining followers on social media) can stack up to newer, bigger wins (like getting a bunch of leads from a Facebook group). Those wins stack up to even bigger wins, like scoring a major client or selling out your newest course.

Start thinking about what small wins you've had this week that you can snowball into bigger wins.

(Pssst... This is where the "map" part of mapping out your wins comes in.)

Let's say your small win this week was meeting another business owner at a networking event.

Depending on your business goals, your map could look like any of these:

New contact → Connect via LinkedIn → Join their network and send some cold pitches

New contact → Invite them to join your Facebook group → They refer new business to you

New contact → Follow up with them in a week to meet in real life → They connect you to other businesses in the area

While snowballing those wins is reason enough to start mapping them

out, there's an even better reason out there: that list of wins is proof of
your success!

Every time I'm on a call with a potential lead, I keep my list handy.
That way, when they ask for concrete examples of my skills, I have
immediate, relevant evidence.

A win is a win, no matter how small.

You should celebrate every single one as evidence of your hard work!

I worked hard to stack my wins and scored some **BIG** ones! Starting
my podcast was a win, running campaigns for influencers was a win,
and being featured in Forbes twice was very cool, too!

You can check out my Forbes articles about the top tips for each social
media platform. Download all resources at
www.HashtagExpertBook.com/resources

I can't wait to help you stack those wins!

How are you going to snowball your wins?

CHAPTER FIFTEEN
HACKS TO HELP YOU OUT

When you are trying to be seen as the expert in your industry, it's important that you position yourself that way. A great way to do this is to get in front of media. Book yourself on podcasts, radio, and TV segments. Guest blog for others and link the blog back to a freebie that you offer that requires your audience to opt-in.

Making great partnerships in the industry also helps a lot. Decide who in the industry is working with people who could also be YOUR people, so that you can share the audience and provide value to them without stepping on anyone's toes.

For example, if you are a health chef, you could guest blog on a health coach's blog. The health coach will teach their audience about living a healthy lifestyle and you would teach about making the menu and how to prepare high-quality foods.

Your audience needs what you both offer but since you don't do the same thing for them, you won't be competing, and you'll be creating an environment of trust. Consumers like partnerships and it boosts both of your expert status' when you can work together to offer high-quality products that your audience needs. It also builds your brand and that will likely get you recommendations and referrals.

You need to remember that there are buyers everywhere and just because they buy from one person doesn't mean they won't buy from another. Think about consumers. We buy a lot of things from a lot of people. So, think of who you could partner with and reach out to them to see if you can guest blog for their site.

Remember to start with value. Offer a lot of value that you can contribute to their site. In return, you will be perceived as the authority just by being featured on someone else's blog and you will grow your list by simply adding a link to your offer at the bottom of your guest blog. This will send the target audience back to your page.

HARO, which stands for Help A Reporter Out (www.helpareporter.com), is a great tool that I've used for years. It's a free service that connects reporters to experts by industry and is an excellent way to get media attention, provide value, and position yourself as the expert.

You can get a daily digest or receive emails three times daily. Sift through the posts in the email for your industry and if something jumps out at you, apply to be featured.

As an example:

A few weeks ago, SUCCESS Magazine was looking for "3 female entrepreneurs for pay negotiation story". If you are a female entrepreneur with a story about how you negotiated for pay, you would click on the link in the email and see the requirements and deadline. It would look something like this:

Query:

I'm looking to interview three female entrepreneurs for a regular "how to" column. This piece will cover personal experiences asking for more money in a business setting. That could include anything from a salary negotiation, business deal, negotiating lower product costs, etc.

Ideally, I'd like to interview women in several different career stages. I'd like to hear from both the positive and negative experiences of financial negotiations, and how those experiences shaped your personal and professional life.

This piece will appear in print as well as online. Headshots to accompany the piece. Thanks!

Requirements:

I would prefer entrepreneurs, small business owners, side gig enthusiasts, etc. I'm not as keen for corporate or C-suite execs, but exceptions can be made for the right story.

There are literally thousands of inquiries daily so take advantage of them and get seen in the media!!

Another great tool I use is Google Alerts. You can set up an alert for anything related to your industry. So, for example, I get Google Alerts for "Facebook" and "Social Media" daily.

Google will send me emails alerting me when these trending topics appear in media. When a big story hits, I know that I can provide value to stay relevant. A great tip I recently learned is that you can Google Alert your name and your company name and see when your business is trending and what people are saying about it.

One of the coolest days in my business was when I was featured in Forbes about Social Media and the Google Alert I received had my article at the top. Thousands of people who receive "social media" alerts saw that in their inbox that day. It was pretty surreal.

(Higher quality images can be found at HashtagExpertBook.com/resources)

Remember to stay relevant in your space and build relationships and partnerships to get visible. If you aren't getting visible, it's like you don't exist.

It's like that age-old question, "If a tree falls in the middle of the woods and nobody hears it, did it make a sound?"

Let's apply that to online business. You have this business, you think it's awesome (of course you do, it's your biz), you know it provides a solution to your target's problem, but you don't show up online everywhere people look.... so, do you even have a business?

If you want people to know you exist, you've got to get visible!

You need to put yourself out there if you want your target market to see you and notice you.

Post consistently, go live, talk about your biz EVERYWHERE, get in groups, build connections, network, hang out where your dream customer is hanging out, and provide value.

Providing value should be one of your top priorities as a business owner.

There is no better way to build an audience than providing constant value, therefore establishing yourself as an expert in your field.

A good ratio to follow is that for every 5 posts you make on social media, only one of them should be sales-based and the rest should be value-based.

Once you get into the habit of doing these things consistently, you will see how much of an impact you can make online and your target audience will find you!

CHAPTER SIXTEEN
WHAT'S NEXT?

I've covered a lot in this book about how you can make a huge impact online and show up as an authority in your industry. Getting #expert status isn't easy, but it is simple. Follow these strategies and you will see that your business really flourishes online.

Keep in mind that the snowball effect is a real thing. You will work day-in and day-out to position yourself properly but as long as you keep on going, the momentum will build, and you will get to a point where the hard work you are putting in will yield huge results.

The trick is in the consistency. Once you stop, it takes twice as much effort to build up the momentum again, so keep going and remember why you are doing this. If you really want to be the industry leader, you need to play like one. The hard work and effort won't equal the results at first, but that's okay. Eventually it will, and the systems you've put in place will run on autopilot. Just keep on keeping on, as they say.

The key is to gain exposure in every avenue possible and get clients that are in alignment with what you offer and believe in. If you are attracting the wrong audience, you need to think about your message, branding, and where you are spending the most time. Shift things around and be flexible if need be. Being flexible in life and in business will open up countless doors. You never know which gate the winning horse will come from, so keep your options open.

Moving forward, I invite you to take advantage of my great resources to help you get started.

Visit www.HashtagExpertBook.com/resources to download all resources for free that were mentioned in this book.

"Finding Your Dream Customer Guide"

Want to get in front of the right audience? Do you know who your marketing is speaking to? You need to design EVERYTHING you say and do online for that ideal client.

"30 Days Of Content Ideas To Kill It On Social Media"

Want to get visible but don't know how much content to create? Do you ever stare at a blank screen unsure of what to write? Never have this problem again.

"4 Emails You Must Send To Your Subscribers To Make Them Love You"

Don't know the importance of having an email list? Or maybe you know the benefits but don't know how to grow your list. Perhaps you have a list, but they don't engage with you or buy your products and services. Having a growing and thriving list is how you have a growing and thriving business. Use this guide and watch your list grow!

Social Marketing Academy!

Join my Social Marketing Academy! It was built to help small business owners and entrepreneurs learn essential skills for growing their business online. This is the nitty-gritty, secret knowledge from a Facebook Ad Expert and Online Marketing Strategist that you'll need to be successful on social media.

Marketing Tips With Meliss Podcast

For more marketing tips, check out my podcast:

www.HashtagExpertBook.com/resources

and give the podcast some love by subscribing and sharing it with those you know who can also benefit!

Magnetic Marketing Mastermind

Join my free Facebook group where I share lots of tips and advice on how to market your business successfully! I'm in the community daily to answer your questions! www.HashtagExpertBook.com/resources

Keep chiseling away at your dream to become an expert in your industry. Just by reading this book, you are already on your way!

You can do it. I believe in you.

RESOURCES: Visit www.HashtagExpertBook.com/resources to download all resources for free that were mentioned in this book, including clickable versions of the links below.

How To Identify Your Strengths
www.oprah.com/inspiration/how-to-identify-your-strengths

Recommendations Most Credible Advertising
www.nielsen.com/us/en/press-room/2015/recommendations-from-friends-remain-most-credible-form-of-advertising.html

www.influenster.com

www.bzzagent.com

#worldstoughestjob
www.youtube.com/watch?v=HB3xM93rXbY&feature=youtu.be

#PutAShirtOn
https://mic.com/articles/189522/fruit-of-the-looms-new-putashirton-campaign-hilariously-puts-dudes-shirtless-selfies-on-blast#.EcqXJIvzp

Ikea Pee Ad
www.adweek.com/creativity/ikea-wants-you-to-pee-on-this-ad-if-youre-pregnant-it-will-give-you-a-discount-on-a-crib

Saying YES! to your Weirdness - JP Sears
https://www.youtube.com/watch?v=79zra755WgA

Outgrow
https://outgrow.co/blog/infographic-science-behind-virality

Top Social Media Tips: Part 1
www.forbes.com/sites/kateharrison/2018/07/02/top-social-media-tips-for-every-platform-part-1-facebook-twitter-and-instagram

Top Social Media Tips: Part 2
www.forbes.com/sites/kateharrison/2018/07/06/top-social-media-tips-for-every-platform-part-2-youtube-linkedin-snapchat-and-pinterest

HARO
www.helpareporter.com

ABOUT THE AUTHOR

Meliss Jakubovic is a Facebook Ad Expert, Online Marketing Strategist, owner of Meliss Marketing in Atlanta, GA, and the founder of the Social Marketing Academy. Her clients, ranging from bakeries and authors to online coaches and influencers, rely on her to put them right in front of their dream customers. She is known as the Lead Generation Genie.

Meliss has created hundreds of sales funnels, managed accounts with over 300k followers, and run ad campaigns for accounts with over $500k ad spend. She travels around the country speaking on stages about her life, business, and success.

Her free Facebook group, Magnetic Marketing Mastermind, provides major value to entrepreneurs and marketers alike.

Business owners look to Meliss to provide them with high-ROI Facebook ads, sales funnels, content creation, list building, and social media visibility.

When she's not helping clients or teaching her SMA students how to make a major impact online, she spends her time doing yoga, DJing, folk dancing, and raising her two children, Shai and Ilan.

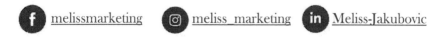

melissmarketing   meliss_marketing   Meliss-Jakubovic

Made in the USA
Columbia, SC
22 February 2021